A Croco-BITE Smile

Jan Burchett and Sara Vogler ● Jon Stuart

Contents

OXFORD
UNIVERSITY PRESS

Macro Marvel
(billionaire inventor)

Welcome to Micro World!

Macro Marvel invented Micro World – a micro-sized theme park where you have to shrink to get in.

A computer called **CODE** controls Micro World and all the robots inside – MITEs and BITEs.

A MITE

A BITE

Disaster strikes!

CODE goes wrong on opening day.
CODE wants to shrink the world.

Macro Marvel is trapped inside the park …

Enter Team X!

Four micro agents – **Max, Cat, Ant** and **Tiger** – are sent to rescue Macro Marvel and defeat CODE.

Mini Marvel joins Team X.

Mini Marvel
(Macro's daughter)

In the last book ...

* Max and Ant set off to rescue Cat and Tiger.
* Max and Ant got stuck in a tunnel so Max used his power mitts to get free.
* Max was dragged out of the boat by the Croco-BITE!

**CODE key
(6 collected)**

You are in the Fiendish Falls zone.

3

Before you read

Sound checker

Say the sounds.

o   oo   ou

Sound spotter

Blend the sounds.

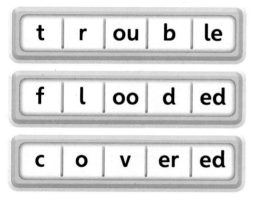

| t | r | ou | b | le |

| f | l | oo | d | ed |

| c | o | v | er | ed |

Tricky words

through
thought

Into the zone

How do you think Max will
escape from the Croco-BITE?

4

Max in Trouble

Mini and Rex saw the Croco-BITE pulling Max through the reeds. "Max is in trouble," thought Mini. "We're coming to help!" she called.

The Croco-BITE flicked its tail. It hit the water and made some big waves. It nearly flooded the river bank.

A couple of waves flooded Mini's boat and covered the bottom. Mini struggled to stop the boat sinking.

The Croco-BITE flicked its tail
again. Max flew through the air!
The BITE was right underneath
him. Its mouth was open wide.

Max quickly shrank and tumbled down into the BITE's hungry mouth! He just missed its long, sharp teeth.

"Rex, how can we help Max now?" gasped Mini.

Now you have read ...
Max in Trouble

Take a closer look

Why did Max shrink?

How did Max end up in the Croco-BITE's mouth?

Where is the rest of Team X?

Who can help Max escape from the Croco-BITE?

What might Max be thinking now?

When do you think Max will find the CODE key?

Thinking time

Who do you think has been the bravest in the Fiendish Falls zone?

Before you read

Sound checker

Say the sounds.

o   oo   ou

Sound spotter

Blend the sounds.

| c | ou | p | le |

| f | l | oo | d |

| c | o | m | f | or | t |

Tricky words

thought
through

Into the zone

Can you remember where the
CODE key is?

Teeth Trap

Max sat up on the Croco-BITE's tongue. "I'm in trouble!" he thought.

Max looked at the row of sharp teeth. One looked strange – it was the CODE key.

Suddenly, the BITE opened its mouth. Water flooded in and swept Max backwards.

Max swam through the flood and reached the tooth. He tugged at it but the Croco-BITE's tongue flicked back and trapped him.

Back in the boat, Mini suddenly saw some swoopies carrying snacks. "Help!" she called. "The BITE has got my friend."

The swoopies saw Max inside the BITE's mouth. They flew down and dropped the snacks on the Croco-BITE's head!

Max saw his chance. He tugged at the tooth a couple of times.

The CODE key popped out and the Croco-BITE stopped.

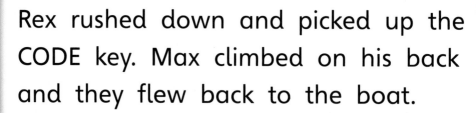

Rex rushed down and picked up the CODE key. Max climbed on his back and they flew back to the boat.

"Well done, Max!" said Mini.
"That was far too close for comfort," said Max.
"Let's find the others and get out of here," said Mini.

Max, Mini and Rex found the others at the top of the falls.

"Come on," said Ant. "We have to go down the Fiendish Flume first."

"That was amazing!" said Max, "but I'm ready for dry land now ..."

Now you have read ...
Teeth Trap

To get to the next zone we have to read the CODE words. Then the exit door will open. Can you help us read them?

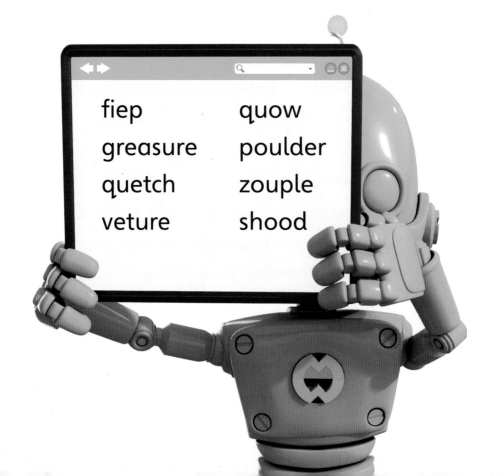

fiep   quow

greasure   poulder

quetch   zouple

veture   shood